Freedom: Deliverance Of Souls From Captivity

Johannes Tefo

Published by Johannes Tefo, 2024.

Also by Johannes Tefo

Family spiritual Warfare Books
Generational Curses And Spiritual Warfare: Spiritual Strategies &
Principles Of Victory Against Evil Strongholds
Youth's Guide To Spiritual Warfare
A Women's Guide To Spiritual Warfare

Standalone
Deliver Your Soul From Evil
Overcoming Spirit Of Stagnation
The 24: Prophetic Word For This Season 2024 And Beyond
Michael For Warfare
Territorial Spirits: Overcome Evil Strongholds in Your Life And
Take Over Your Community With Strategic Warfare And
Winning Prayers
Prayers Against Suicide Spirit
Spiritual Warfare When Enough is Enough
Identity In Christ
Prayers Against Satanic Networks

The Workplace You Need: Spiritual Warfare Prayers That Silence Evil Powers At Your Workplace.

Deliverance From Mind Control: Be Free And Delivered From Every Marine Demons Of Mind Control

Times Getting Hard: Scriptures Of Comfort For Hard Days

Battle In The Sea: How To Tackle Spiritual Warfare And Win The Battle

Freedom: Deliverance Of Souls From Captivity

Table of Contents

Dedicated to every soul in need of a Reedemer. Christ is enough!

He came to set the captives free.

―――

Jeremiah 33:7 And I will cause the captivity of Judah and the captivity of Israel to return,

and will build them, as at the first.

As for thee also, BY THE BLOOD of thy covenant I have sent forth thy

prisoners out of the pit wherein there is no water.

Zech. 9:11

You will never know captivity until you are in prison. You will never know the power of healing until you are ill yourself. For most of us in this school of life, experience is the best teacher. We are in school, we are in training, we know in part. The more you know in a certain area, the more you walk in power in that area.

I was called to write about my testimony of deliverance by the LORD. I have been in the darkness—darkness almost covered my soul. By the grace of the light of GOD, light always arises in the darkness. This is the GOD we serve. Who in most cases is the redeemer in the last hour. When they are celebrating in the kingdom of darkness for capturing your soul, at the last minute He appears as a mighty warrior.

When GOD arises, His enemies fall like drunkard men. The hand of GOD reaches even the foundation of hell itself. He doesn't shake the earth but the foundation of the earth. darkness cannot win against darkness; it is the light that prevails against the power of darkness.

CHRIST is the light of this world. And through CHRIST, we are the light of this world. We are the children of the light. We live in a world covered with darkness. For men have invited darkness to walk among us. Men have made a pact with the powers of darkness—granting these spirits the legal right to do as they please. For their goal is destruction—to kill, steal, and destroy. The same Luciferian agenda.

Psalm 68:18 Thou hast ascended on high, thou hast led captivity captive: thou hast

received gifts for men; yea, for the rebellious also, that the LORD God might

dwell among them.

The death of the cross became the cornerstone of deliverance for many. The people of faith since the beginning of this world, were redeemed by the power of the cross of Christ. As in the days of Moses those who looked upon the golden serpent were healed, and many who looked upon the death of the cross, who believed, were received and delivered from the sting of death.

The prophets prophesied concerning the deliverance the Son of God was to bring, and after Jesus Christ entered into the regions of death and liberated those who were held by its chains, those who had died in the hope of the promise, those who had died in the fullness of faith that the Redeemer was to come.

He came and the actual deliverance from the power of death took place. "He led captivity captive, He ascended up on high" and their place of residence was transferred from that place (Sheol) governed by the power of death and the angel of death to wherever the Lord Jesus Christ went. "They ascended up on high" and their place of residence was changed.

Those who have their residence with the Lord Jesus Christ, from the day of His resurrection and onward, would have to be called down, not up.

Christ brought paradise within our hearts. The life of victory from the power of death. The captives here are the saints of old who died as before Christ no one went to heaven, except two men, Enoch and Elijah.

Genesis 5:21-24 And Enoch lived sixty and five years, and begat Methuselah:

22 And Enoch walked with God after he begat Methuselah three hundred

years, and begat sons and daughters:

23 And all the days of Enoch were three hundred sixty and five years:

24 And Enoch walked with God: and he was not; for God took him.

2 King 2:11 And it came to pass, as they still went on, and talked, that, behold, there

appeared a chariot of fire, and horses of fire, and parted them both asunder; and

Elijah went up by a whirlwind into heaven.

The faith of Enoch and Elijah was so honorable to GOD that He allowed them to depart this world extraordinarily without tasting death. Apart from CHRIST the captives free from the land of the death, the saints of old, this was his commission;

Isaiah 61:12 The Spirit of the Lord GOD is upon me; because the LORD hath anointed

me to preach good tidings unto the meek; he hath sent me to bind up the

brokenhearted, to proclaim liberty to the captives, and the opening of the prison

to them that are bound; 2 To proclaim the acceptable year of the LORD,

On the street of Galilea, the good news was preached. The good news, the gospel of souls, was preached to the end of the world. In a world that was filled with darkness, the light arose illuminating every house that accepted it. The light is the truth of the GOD. Light is knowledge, wisdom, and understanding of the ways of the LORD.

JESUS spoke the light into people's hearts. Spoke the truth to the lie—uprooting it from the core. The foundation of the Devil is only shaken by the truth. Walking in truth will make you to be above the evil system. However, the road is not easy. It is not as easy as some preachers teach.

It is a narrow journey of courage that was spoken into the life of Moses and Joshua,

Deutronomy 34:9-12 And Joshua the son of Nun was full of the spirit of wisdom; for Moses

had laid his hands upon him: and the children of Israel hearkened unto him, and

did as the LORD commanded Moses.

10 And there arose not a prophet since in Israel like unto Moses, whom the

LORD knew face to face,

11 In all the signs and the wonders, which the LORD sent him to do in the

land of Egypt to Pharaoh, and to all his servants, and to all his land,

12 And in all that mighty hand, and in all the great terror which Moses

shewed in the sight of all Israel.

The name Joshua means a deliverer. He was the one to deliver the children of Israel to the promised land—he took off where Moses, the man of GOD left. When you read the Bible from Genesis to Revelation, you realize that it Is a deliverance book. It is about GOD redeeming mankind from the grip of bondage.

From Adam and Eve times, the enemy has been running the show. JESUS who bears the same name as Joshua, also came with the redemption of the blood for mankind—liberating souls from captivity—from demonic strongholds.

He went all about doing good, healing all, and delivering all who were in bondage of sin—tormented by the Devils day and night. JESUS, our Messiah, is the redeemer of all souls, never mind the color. By the way, the soul does not have color. The color of the soul is the light of GOD. Let CHRIST in you be the hope of your salvation.

Deuteronomy 31:7-8And Moses called unto Joshua, and said unto him in the sight of all Israel,

Be strong and of a good courage: for thou must go with this people unto the land

which the LORD hath sworn unto their fathers to give them; and thou shalt cause

them to inherit it.

8 And the LORD, he it is that doth go before thee; he will be with thee, he

will not fail thee, neither forsake thee: fear not, neither be dismayed.

The road to deliverance needs courage and strong character. Deliverance goes beyond the casting of demons. It is a life lived dedicated to GOD and being grateful for being delivered out of the hands of the Evil one.

Ephesians 1:7 In whom we have redemption through his blood, the forgiveness of sins,

The blood of JESUS is potent against the evil powers of the enemy. When we testify who we are in CHRIST and what the blood does in our lives, we have the killer testimony that is deadlier to the kingdom of darkness.

Through pleading the blood of the lamb over my faith journey as a believer, I have seen the forces of darkness overthrown and destroyed. It is all about winning territory in the spirit world. Joshua conquered territory by the hand of the LORD. GOD plays on his part. But you also have to stand up like a mighty warrior and fight for your generation.

This book is a testimony of deliverance. Testimony of redemption. We are all on this journey to liberate ourselves from the school of bondage. In all things, we ought to look upon the CHRIST, as many who looked upon Him were never ashamed.

Psalm 34:5 They looked unto him, and were lightened: and their faces were not

ashamed.

Psalm 34:8 O taste and see that the LORD is good: blessed is the man that trusteth in

him.

Freedom in Christ.

Jeremiah 30:8 For it shall come to pass in that day, saith the LORD of hosts, that I will

break his yoke from off thy neck, and will burst thy bonds, and strangers shall no

more serve themselves of him: 9 But they shall serve the LORD their God, and

David their king, whom I will raise up unto them.

This scripture talks about freedom from slavery, oppression, depression, and more. Through disobedience to the law of CHRIST misfortune has befallen us. Sin opens the door to demons. Demons come with all kinds of affliction and oppression. You are under bondage when evil spirits are pulling strings in your life—influencing you will all kinds of lies.

Freedom in CHRIST is knowing that your soul is secured in the books of life at the end of the race. It is the absence of fear of the unknown. However, through the working of the HOLY SPIRIT, we know that beyond the curtains of time, there is life. In CHRIST, we are rest assured of our eternal souls to be with Him when we depart.

Jeremiah 33:6 Behold, I will bring it health and cure, and I will cure them, and will reveal unto them the abundance of peace and truth.

Freedom in CHRIST goes beyond the achievement of material things and the peace of mind. It is a guarantee of His mercy, His love, and His grace for our souls. We have to know that the enemy is after our souls more than anything. Satan can make you a Billionaire overnight just to snatch your soul. He is the soul snatcher!

I was listening to an interview on a certain television network, and this high-profile movie star said "When I had money, I bought all the things that I wanted, did all the things I wanted to the point where I did them all that I did not know what to do next".

You realize how much you need something but once you get all that you want, you start questioning yourself like "What's next?". I for one, believe that material things should come with spiritual maturity. Blessings from the LORD GOD adds no sorrow. If your blessings add sorrows to your life, my friend, the Devil is at play.

Freedom in CHRIST is the transformed mind from an earthy point of view to the heavenly plane. You know you are free when you start seeing things from GOD's perspective rather than from a human view. GOD'S view is infinite. Man's view is limited.

Moses was commanded by the LORD GOD to tell the children of Israel to slaughter a lamb without blemish of one year for their Passover, and with its blood to be sprinkled upon the doorposts for their deliverance from the Angel of death. The blood of the lamb delivered the whole nation from the plague of death.

Note that the death was even going to be upon the firstborn of everything, men and Animals. Animals at that time were the weight of their wealth. Cows, goats, sheep Carmel, etc., represent wealth. The LORD protected their lives and their wealth. CHRIST is the Passover lamb that still speaks through His blood in our families. The blood of the LAMB always speaks better things—and it is a better covenant.

The involvement of Satan in the corruption of man makes it humanly impossible for man to free himself. There is no accused person, who can post bail for himself. Every time you are caught up in sin, you are under arrest. You need a recognized authority to bail you.

The Blood of Jesus is that authority! The blood of Jesus is your guarantee for bail. It offers you the privilege of being discharged and acquitted so that you can walk in liberty all the days of your life.

True freedom requires divine intervention. Your freedom must therefore have its roots in Christ, and in the things that are provided for your liberty. Then you will be complete in Him. It is time for the Church to be complete, and we can only be complete in Him in the provisions He has made, not in our abilities and expertise.

The divine blood of CHRIST is a provision for man's freedom from every satanic dimension of corruption. It is what it takes to silence the opposition. It is the ultimate for our victory. We overcome by the blood of the lamb and by testifying the power of the blood to situations.

Through the power of the blood of the lamb, you will be able to cross over from bondage to liberty, from death to life, from degradation to beautification, and from pains to ease.

Freedom from sin.

The first freedom we can talk about is forgiveness of sin. Sin separated men from GOD. CHRIST restored man and woman to Eden by taking away our sins by His death. Now we can hear the voice of the HOLY SPIRIT when He is talking. The separation is restored. Glory to CHRIST who has given us the greatest gift and assurance to our spirit, soul, and body when we depart.

Without Holiness, we cannot see the face of GOD. Our ticket to holiness is CHRIST himself. He is the only way to the Father.

Colossians 1:12-14 Giving thanks unto the Father, which hath made us meet to be partakers

of the inheritance of the saints in light:

13 Who hath delivered us from the power of darkness, and hath translated us

into the kingdom of his dear Son:

14 In whom we have redemption through his blood, even the forgiveness of

sins:

We are no longer in darkness, we are the inheritors of light along with the saints. Throughout my Christian walk, I have almost met every biblical figure of the bible. These are the saints of light who are also called the cloud of witnesses, who intercede for the believers to hold onto faith till the end of the race.

Hebrews 12:1 Wherefore seeing we also are compassed about with so great a cloud of

witnesses, let us lay aside every weight, and the sin which doth so easily beset

us, and let us run with patience the race that is set before us,

As much as angels are sent forth to minister to us, these saints, also point us to CHRIST, the author and the finisher of our faith. I have seen Paul, Abraham, Jacob, Judah, David, Joshua, Elijah, Samuel, Elisha, Daniel, and many more. I believe every believer who has a deep relationship with CHRIST, CHRIST has revealed Himself unto him or her.

CHRIST can descend from his throne for you, just to see you. As much as He can send His angels down here, in most cases, He will appear unto you. That's how special you are. He can shift the mountain just to see you. In the old days, He opened the rivers so that Moses and his people could pass through. In Babylon, He quenched the fire so that Shadrack, Meshach, and Abednego could live.

King Nebuchadnezzar saw the Son of the LIVING GOD in the fiery fire. The LORD who is consuming fire could not be flamed by it. The life of these three men is a testament to tried faith. Faith not tried cannot grow. We can also talk about Daniel, whom the lions did not kill because Daniel is a lion himself. He is from the tribe of Judah—represented by a lion. In this stance, we still see the mighty hand of GOD. In the old days, the angel of the presence of GOD was CHRIST himself. CHRIST manifested expressly before time.

He has been our redeemer since the beginning. Here is what David says "The *LORD said unto my Lord, Sit thou at my right hand, until I make thine enemies thy footstool*".

We have the great high priest of the new covenant who offered Himself as the blood sacrifice for many. Redemption of any kind is in JESUS.

Isaiah 53:3-5 He is despised and rejected of men; a man of sorrows, and acquainted

with grief: and we hid as it were our faces from him; he was despised, and we

esteemed him not.

4 Surely he hath borne our griefs, and carried our sorrows: yet we did

esteem him stricken, smitten of God, and afflicted.

5 But he was wounded for our transgressions, he was bruised for our

iniquities: the chastisement of our peace was upon him; and with his stripes we

are healed.

Your iniquity was laid on the cross. Your griefs and sorrows, JESUS took. The lashes and beating He received were our healing. *with his stripes we are healed.*

There is no greater deliverance story than the story of the cross. The man was reconciled to GOD. The veil was unveiled. The real Jerusalem was the body of JESUS. His spirit still indwells us; thus we are called the temple of the HOLY SPIRIT. In the flesh of His body, He has reconciled us to the Father.

Through the death of Jesus, the slavery ended. Through the blood of Jesus, access is now provided for all into the Holy of Holies. Everyone now has access to the things behind the veil, not only for discoveries but much more importantly, to see the goodness of the LORD.

Colossians 1:20-22 And, having made peace through the blood of his cross, by him to

reconcile all things unto himself; by him, I say, whether they be things in earth,

or things in heaven.

21 And you, that were sometime alienated and enemies in your mind by

wicked works, yet now hath he reconciled

22 In the body of his flesh through death, to present you holy and

unblameable and unreproveable in his sight:

Freedom from mental illness.

Mental and physical illness can be the result of demonic oppression. By the spirit of GOD, we can know about the roots if something is of the devil or nature. Some things need a natural remedy, and there is something that needs pastoral attention, which is deliverance. Depression, ADHD, Schizophrenia, personality disorder, and many other mental issues can be healed in the name of JESUS.

There are countless testimonies of brothers and sisters who were healed from these mental issues. JESUS is the greatest healer you can have in your life if you believe.

Mark 11:24 Therefore I say unto you, What things soever ye desire, when ye pray,

believe that ye receive them, and ye shall have them.

Through faith, the impossible is possible. Through faith, the incurable are curable. Through faith, we shall surely do valiant things in the name of the LORD.

Mark 11:23 For verily I say unto you, That whosoever shall say unto this mountain,

Be thou removed, and be thou cast into the sea; and shall not doubt in his heart,

but shall believe that those things which he saith shall come to pass; he shall

have whatsoever he saith.

For those who suffer from depression, anxiety, Schizophrenia, and other mental illnesses, there is hope and recovery.

Jeremiah 30:17 For I will restore health unto thee, and I will heal thee of thy wounds,

Proclaim your healing through holy communion. Speak healing words unto the wounds of your heart. Like a mighty warrior, let the high praises of GOD be in your mouth—singing that you are healed even if you are not. You should believe it before you see it. David knew of the victory before the fight with Goliath. He was not intimidated by the height of Goliath. We shouldn't be intimated by what we see with our own eyes. GOD IS BIG!

With all kinds of prayer, we should earnestly seek the face of the LORD. I wrote the called *Demons Behind Schizophrenia*, this was my autobiography or testimony of healing from mental illness—Schizophrenia. And I have written the steps that took me from bondage to freedom.

I am a healthy young man. All glory unto the LORD. Throughout those years when I was hearing voices, I would pray and fast regularly. I made sure that always the bible was beside me. Day and night I will meditate on the scriptures—especially scriptures pertaining to healing and faith.

These are the weapons of warfare that destroyed the evil powers of stronghold;

- Praise and worship.
- Prayer and fasting.
- Scripture meditation.
- Thanksgiving.

- The blood of JESUS!

Many are bound by demons—solving demonic issues with medication. One of the greatest slave-ship of mankind is ignorance of the Word of GOD. We are in darkness when we ignore the voice of the HOLY SPIRIT and the Word of GOD. A few days ago, I heard the voice of the HOLY SPIRIT.

Freedom from mind control

Apart from bondage being in your skin, on a larger scale it can affect your mind. Yes, the battle is in your mind. The evil one is targeting your mind to keep you hostage of believing the lie. After the truth comes the peace of mind. The lie is confusion, manipulation, and deception. These are the fiery darts of the enemy.

You cannot know the truth if you have ever been told a lie all your life. It takes the greater power of GOD to destroy the strongholds of the lie and replace it with the truth. The truth is the person of JESUS. The lie is the Devil.

In the gifting of the HOLY SPIRIT, there is a special gift called the discerning of spirits. If you are truly in CHRIST, this gift will help you to discern both good and evil. Personally, this gift has saved me from many obstacles.

It is more like your intuition; you just know what you know that you know. It is spiritual enlightenment concerning current issues. The gift covers the whole spectrum of word of wisdom, word of knowledge, and understanding.

The HOLY SPIRIT in you will help you and lead you away from things that are not of GOD. Mind control is evil. We are called to have the same mind that JESUS had—the mind of CHRIST.

For those who are in battleship with occult mind control, JESUS is the answer. The blood of JESUS is the answer. The Word of GOD is the answer. Scripture meditation is the key. The Word is powerful. The Word is sharper than a two-edged sword. The Word is the sword of the spirit.

You are sure on your way to victory if you can defeat the enemy of your mind. Your thoughts speak louder than your words. We ought to look above where lies our destiny. Our heritage is the kingdom of GOD that is above, and that is also within us. Therefore, the transformed mind is vital for our character, vision, and dreams.

Romans 12:2 And be not conformed to this world: but be ye transformed by the

renewing of your mind, that ye may prove what is that good, and acceptable, and

perfect, will of God.

It is on our part to ensure we are transformed into the mind of CHRIST through the Word. The system, culture, and traditions of this world, are against the will and the mind of GOD. Loving the things of this world and partaking in them is an enmity to GOD. GOD is above our system. The system of GOD is His word period.

If you know the truth, you cannot be easily deceived. The truth shall set you free. During the trial of JESUS CHRIST, the leader of that time asked him "What is the truth", and he answered, "I am the truth". The truth is the light. The truth is the way. The truth is life. These are but the facets of CHRIST.

Be transformed into the truth of GOD through mirroring his word. We move from glory to glory when He is in us.

Psalm 1:2-3But his delight is in the law of the LORD; and in his law doth he meditate

day and night.

3 And he shall be like a tree planted by the rivers of water, that bringeth

forth his fruit in his season; his leaf also shall not wither; and whatsoever he

doeth shall prosper.

FREEDOM FROM FEAR.

The greatest weapon the enemy ever plagued a man with is fear. Fear derailed the dreams and destinies of many if not millions upon millions. Fear is spiritual. If we do not treat it from a spiritual standpoint, we will greatly suffer the defeat of this crippling fear. However, there is a natural fear such as being intimidated in an interview or driving for a fast time. Naturally in these settings, you can be intimidated.

It gets even harder when you are bound by fear. There are many who are living proof that fear is a spirit. And you cannot wholeheartedly trust in the promises of GOD while in the sinking ship of fear. From time to time spirit of GOD encourages His servant to take courage. The fearful are those who do not have courage. Courage is power—the unshakable truth of GOD.

Scripture says that the righteous are as bold as lions. Fear will keep you from dreaming. Fear will keep you in the shackles of non-achievement life. Fear will keep you from experiencing the goodness of the LORD.

Psalm 34:8 O taste and see that the LORD is good: blessed is the man that trusteth in

him.

The goodness of the LORD comes with the peace of mind. The goodness of the LORD comes with unshakable faith. While the opposite of faith is fear. Don't get it twisted, there is a natural fear. And a fear of the demonic realm.

I wrote about mind control in the previous chapter. Many who are also spiritually bound mentally, experience demonic fear. It is even played out in their dream life. At night, they are bombarded with scary dreams and visions—nightmares.

There is deliverance in the house of GOD. The house of GOD is the house of prayer. Staying in the Word not only impacts your spiritual life but also your mental issues. The issues of the mind are as important as the issue of the spirit. There is total freedom in everything, even the deepest addictions can be alleviated.

Who am I in Christ?

This is a deep question. Who art though? And many of us tend to conclude what we like and don't like to make up our persona. We base this answer according to our personality and identity imputed by external factors. And in most cases, personality is built up by external factors. The music we listen to, the clothes we wear, the careers we choose, the circle of friends we hang out with, and so on.

This is the same question the Pharisees sent their soldiers to ask John the Baptist "Who art thou"? since John knew who he was, he answered them in the light of the scriptures *"I am The voice of one crying in the wilderness, Prepare ye the way of the Lord, make his paths straight"*.

The purpose and destiny of John was revealed by the hand of angels. It goes to say, that if you want to know who you are, allow the Holy Spirit to reveal who you are. John found himself when he read Isaiah 40:3.

JESUS CHRIST found himself in the scripture Isaiah 61:1. It is in light of the Word of GOD that mirrors our purpose and destinies in life. When we look deep within ourselves enough, we can come out with a fully verged testimony of who we are.

While many go around this world looking for validation from the outside world—we look within where lies the endless possibilities. Holy Spirit is your friend. GOD left a holy mark in our hearts so that we can bear witness to His goodness. John the Baptist was filled with the Holy Ghost even before birth.

The spirit of power in the life of John sustained him and molded him into the great man of GOD he was. CHRIST holds John above all prophets who ever lived. It is the spirit of humility, grace, and power that earned John the prestige as the last great prophet of the bible. But there would not be John if there was not Elijah. The prophetic line of Elijah to Elisha, and lastly to John, is the prophetic office of power that concerns itself with righteousness and holiness.

John did not look at his physical appearance, or rather, allow the external factor to dictate who he was. The greatest shift in his life happened when he broke away from the normal tradition of staying in the synagogue of that time, or Jerusalem for the service of priesthood. He went to the wilderness and encountered the Most High. If he had to comfortably enjoy the priestly benefits of being a Levi in the temple of Jerusalem, he would have never realized his calling.

Like many of us, we living other people's calling. We are validated by others, neglecting our core values and GOD-given dreams that we should have embarked on years ago—taking the less road traveled.

GOD is looking for those who will allow the Holy Spirit to mold them into who they are supposed to be.

Psalm 100:3 Know ye that the LORD he is God: it is he that hath made

us, and not we ourselves; we are his people, and the sheep of his pasture.

Knowing the fact that we come from the LORD will save us from many troubles and direct our life paths according to the roots we stem from. GOD is spirit. The spirit part of ourselves is as important as much as we care about the body. Spirit keeps the body going. If you can know the fullness of your spirit, you will know that you are capable of anything. We know that we can do anything through Christ.

We also learn about the importance of words; that words are spirit. Words, thoughts, and imaginations are powerhouse you have to direct your path in line with the destiny of GOD. In CHRIST, we have the mind of CHRIST. The spirit man is the real man. Nourishing the real man within, you shall see the power of GOD and His grace abound in your life.

Apostle Peter knew himself as the rock after an encounter with CHRIST. This is what we call life destiny. Fishermen we turned into fishers of men. We can also look at the greatest Apostle, Paul, it was only after an encounter with JESUS CHRIST that he knew his lifetime mission—taking the gospel of Jesus CHRIST to the world. When you come to GOD, He reveals who you are. You do not have to waste time looking at who you are outside of the Godhead.

GOD is first and foremost. Education cannot give you a godly identity. A good paying job will not also help you find yourself. You first understand that you are a spirit. And as a spirit, your hungry spirit needs to be fed with spiritual food to fully function to the best of your ability. GOD is that energy source to give light to your spirit man. Christ is the way, truth, and life you will ever need. You start to learn that you were born with the spirit of power. Here is what the Psalmist had to say,

Psalm 8:2 Out of the mouth of babes and sucklings hast thou ordained

strength

because of thine enemies, that thou mightest still the enemy and the

avenger.

How much more do we need when even out of the mouth of babes comes power? Children of GOD are ordained with the power to silence the works of the darkness. We have Christ who has triumphed over ancient powers of evil that have been holding us hostage for so long.

Let us be for CHRIST. We are living in difficult times whereby media is slowly destroying the real identity of men and women. We are buying into this worldly culture that is destroying our souls every day. The real success is determined by how your Instagram page looks, or how much following you have on overall social media. While in the background folks are depressed and suicidal in keeping up with the social demands. GOD help us!

Identity issues are what keep many from taking action—reaching their destinies. The life of John the Baptist was revealed by Angel Gabriel to his parents; the name, office, and his function. I also believe that his parents played a huge role in his identity. The fact that in due time, he left his native to lodge in the wilderness, was a testament to the spirit of Elijah at play at that point.

The family has a role to play in our call of GOD. We see in the life of Abraham, that GOD called him out of his native for a different path. GOD wanted to have a special relationship with Abraham, and He wouldn't in Haran because of its idolatry. Before He could have a serious walk with Gideon, GOD told him to destroy the idol of his father's house; altars of Baal and Ashtoreth.

You will have to lose something to gain CHRIST. Peter lost His fisherman job. Many have lost their family for following CHRIST. Even some, have lost their lives for the call of CHRIST. CHRIST is worth more than gold and diamonds combined. CHRIST's treasures are eternal. You cannot miss eternal bliss for temporal enjoyment. Folks, we can still enjoy what life has to offer even in the house of prayer. The kingdom of GOD is the government of prayer.

Parents in the LORD can get you so far in the things of the LORD. Like Samuel, you have to stand up on your own and be your generation. Priest Eli can teach you about the ways of the LORD but the future lies in your hands to inspire your generation.

Moses was the greatest prophet who ever lived but there came a time when he had to leave this earth. Joshua was the man to be ordained into the prophetic office of Moses, the man of GOD. Joshua had to be strong, man up, and lead his generation through faith. While people are not replaceable, through faith, men and women can do valiant things.

While you might be submitting under a certain ministry, it is also a good thing to develop your faith and relationship with your GOD in a secret place. Your altar in the secret place will sustain you. No man can sustain you but the spirit of the Living GOD. This goes to my African brothers and sisters in the LORD. It all comes down to identity in the LORD. Do what GOD has called you to do, not what your Pastor calls you to do.

Humility is great but only under the leadership of the Holy Spirit. It does not do good to respect the culture we are in while neglecting the mighty GOD, who is above all, and in all.

Psalm 82:6 I have said, Ye are gods; and all of you are children of the most

High.

Scripture cannot be broken. This scripture says "Ye are gods". The spirit in you is Holy as it is the breath from the Holy mouth of the Holy Father. You are the child of the Most High GOD. This is the identity you bear, and it will never change. This is your first DNA. We also draw power from the blood of CHRIST. While other pagan religions strengthen themselves with the blood of animals, we pride ourselves on the precious blood of the lamb as the real testament of victory over our lives. GOD is great folks!

See yourself how GOD sees you. See yourself in CHRIST. See yourself complete. Walking in the perfection of CHRIST through faith. It can only be through the faith of Abraham that we can please GOD. Life is great when you are all about pleasing GOD rather than men. You cannot please men and win this race called life. Take heart. Be courageous like Joshua.

In Christ 100 Prayer points

1. In Christ, I am chosen and predestined to be holy and blameless before God. (Ephesians 1:4)

2. In Christ, I am a beloved child of God, lavished with His great love. (1 John 3:1)

3. In Christ, I am a new creation; the old has passed away, and the new has come. (2 Corinthians 5:17)

4. In Christ, I am an heir of God and a co-heir with Christ, sharing in His glory. (Romans 8:17)

5. In Christ, I am part of a chosen people, a royal priesthood, and a holy nation. (1 Peter 2:9)

6. In Christ, I am washed, sanctified, and justified by the blood of Jesus. (1 Corinthians 6:11)

7. In Christ, nothing can separate me from the love of God. (Romans 8:38-39)

8. In Christ, I am fearfully and wonderfully made, a masterpiece

of God's creation. (Psalm 139:14)

9. In Christ, I have redemption and the forgiveness of sins.

(Colossians 1:13-14)

10. In Christ, I am crucified with Him, and I now live by faith in

His sacrificial love. (Galatians 2:20)

11. In Christ, I am an ambassador for His kingdom, proclaiming

His message of reconciliation. (2 Corinthians 5:20)

12. In Christ, I am seated with Him in heavenly places, far above
all

powers and authorities. (Ephesians 2:6)

13. In Christ, I am set free from the bondage of sin and
empowered

to walk in righteousness. (Galatians 5:1)

14. In Christ, I am more than a conqueror through Him who loves

me. (Romans 8:37)

15. In Christ, I am transformed by the renewing of my mind,

reflecting His image. (Romans 12:2)

16. In Christ, I am hidden with Him, secure in His love and

protection. (Colossians 3:3)

17. In Christ, my body is a temple of the Holy Spirit, and I honor

God with it. (1 Corinthians 6:19-20)

18. In Christ, I overcome the world by faith, walking in victory and

confidence. (1 John 5:4)

19. In Christ, I am filled with power by the Holy Spirit to be His

witness to the ends of the earth. (Acts 1:8)

20. In Christ, I present myself as an instrument of righteousness,

pleasing to God. (Romans 6:13)

21. In Christ, I am purified and made holy, reflecting His

righteousness. (Titus 2:14)

22. In Christ, I am accepted and included in His family, a fellow

citizen of His kingdom. (Ephesians 2:19)

23. In Christ, I have abundant life, overflowing with His love, joy,

and peace. (John 10:10)

24. In Christ, I am being renewed in knowledge, becoming more

like Him day by day. (Colossians 3:10)

25. In Christ, I am called to be holy as He is holy, set apart for His

purposes. (1 Peter 1:15-16)

26. In Christ, I am blessed with every spiritual blessing in the

heavenly realms. (Ephesians 1:3)

27. In Christ, I am saved and called to live a holy life according to

His purpose and grace. (2 Timothy 1:9)

28. In Christ, I am filled with hope and joy, trusting in His

promises

for my future. (Romans 15:13)

29. In Christ, I am clothed with His righteousness and identified

as

His own. (Galatians 3:27)

30. In Christ, I am destined for glory, sharing in His divine nature

and inheritance. (2 Peter 1:4)

31. In Christ, I am the apple of God's eye, protected and cherished

by Him. (Zechariah 2:8)

32. In Christ, I am restored, strengthened, and established by His

grace. (1 Peter 5:10)

33. In Christ, I shine as a light in the world, reflecting His love and

truth. (Matthew 5:14)

34. In Christ, I hunger and thirst for righteousness, finding

fulfillment in Him. (Matthew 5:6)

35. In Christ, I desire to know Him more deeply, sharing in His

sufferings and resurrection power. (Philippians 3:10)

36. In Christ, I seek first His kingdom and righteousness, finding

true satisfaction and purpose. (Matthew 6:33)

37. In Christ, I am a member of His body, united with other

believers in love and fellowship. (1 Corinthians 12:27)

38. In Christ, I have access to the wisdom of God and the mind of

Christ. (1 Corinthians 2:16)

39. In Christ, I bear the fruit of the Spirit, displaying His love, joy,

peace, and more. (Galatians 5:22-23)

40. In Christ, I am sealed with the Holy Spirit, guaranteed of my

inheritance and salvation. (Ephesians 1:13-14)

41. In Christ, I am rooted and established in His love, filled with

His fullness. (Ephesians 3:17-19)

42. In Christ, I eagerly await His return, knowing that I will be
like

Him when He appears. (1 John 3:2)

43. In Christ, I walk by the Spirit, overcoming the desires of the

flesh and living in freedom. (Galatians 5:16)

44. In Christ, I am justified and sanctified, made righteous and set

apart for His purposes. (Romans 5:1)

45. In Christ, I am reconciled to God and entrusted with the

ministry of reconciliation. (2 Corinthians 5:18)

46. In Christ, I am empowered to stand firm against the schemes
of

the enemy, wielding the armor of God. (Ephesians 6:10-18)

47. In Christ, I am filled with the peace of God, ruling in my heart

and mind. (Philippians 4:7)

48. In Christ, I offer myself as a living sacrifice, holy and pleasing
to

God. (Romans 12:1)

49. In Christ, I am more than a conqueror, facing trials and

tribulations with His strength and courage. (Romans 8:37)

50. In Christ, I am rooted and built up in Him, strengthened in
my

faith and overflowing with thankfulness. (Colossians 2:7)

51. In Christ, I am seated with Him in heavenly places, reigning

with Him in authority and power. (Ephesians 2:6)

52. In Christ, I am confident of His plans and purposes for my

life, knowing that He works all things for my good. (Jeremiah

29:11)

53. In Christ, I am filled with the knowledge of His will, walking
in

wisdom and understanding. (Colossians 1:9)

54. In Christ, I am rooted in love, grounded in His truth, and
filled

with His Spirit. (Ephesians 3:17)

55. In Christ, I am a vessel of His grace and a witness of His love
to

the world. (Acts 1:8)

56. In Christ, I am strengthened with power through His Spirit,

able to do all things through Him who gives me strength.

(Philippians 4:13)

57. In Christ, I am empowered to love others as He has loved me,

bearing His image and reflecting His character. (John

13:34-35)

58. In Christ, I am forgiven of all my sins, washed clean by His

precious blood. (Ephesians 1:7)

59. In Christ, I am called to walk in humility and gentleness, bearing with one another in love. (Ephesians 4:2)

60. In Christ, I am filled with hope and joy, anchored in the promises of His word. (Romans 15:13)

61. In Christ, I am anointed by His Spirit, equipped and empowered to fulfill His purposes. (1 John 2:27)

62. In Christ, I am called to live a life worthy of the calling I have received, bearing fruit in every good work. (Colossians 1:10)

63. In Christ, I am surrounded by His peace, guarding my heart and

mind in Him. (Philippians 4:7)

64. In Christ, I am secure in His love, confident that nothing can separate me from His presence. (Romans 8:38-39)

65. In Christ, I am victorious over every trial and temptation, standing firm in His promises. (1 Corinthians 15:57)

66. In Christ, I am filled with the joy of the Lord, rejoicing in His salvation and goodness. (Psalm 16:11)

67. In Christ, I am called to walk in unity with fellow believers, bearing with one another in love. (Ephesians 4:3)

68. In Christ, I am a living stone, chosen and precious in God's sight, built into a spiritual house. (1 Peter 2:4-5)

69. In Christ, I am strengthened with power through His Spirit, able to endure and persevere through all things. (Ephesians 3:16)

70. In Christ, I am a temple of the Holy Spirit, set apart for His glory and filled with His presence. (1 Corinthians 6:19-20)

71. In Christ, I am called to walk in humility and gentleness, bearing with one another in love. (Ephesians 4:2)

72. In Christ, I am filled with faith, trusting in His promises and believing for His miracles. (Hebrews 11:1)

73. In Christ, I am rooted and grounded in love, rooted in His truth and grounded in His grace. (Ephesians 3:17)

74. In Christ, I am a chosen people, a royal priesthood, a holy nation, God's special possession. (1 Peter 2:9)

75. In Christ, I am a co-heir with Christ, sharing in His inheritance and glory. (Romans 8:17)

76. In Christ, I am called to bear fruit, producing a harvest of

righteousness and love. (John 15:5)

77. In Christ, I am filled with the fruit of the Spirit, walking in

love, joy, peace, patience, kindness, goodness, faithfulness,

gentleness, and self-control. (Galatians 5:22-23)

78. In Christ, I am seated with Him in heavenly places, far above
all

rule and authority, power and dominion. (Ephesians 1:20-21)

79. In Christ, I am redeemed and forgiven, set free from the power

of sin and death. (Ephesians 1:7)

80. In Christ, I am called to be a light in the world, shining His
love

and truth to those around me. (Matthew 5:14)

81. In Christ, I am empowered to overcome every obstacle and

challenge, victorious through His strength. (Philippians 4:13)

82. In Christ, I am filled with His peace, a peace that surpasses all

understanding and guards my heart and mind. (Philippians 4:7)

83. In Christ, I am blessed with every spiritual blessing in the

heavenly realms, chosen and adopted as His child. (Ephesians

1:3)

84. In Christ, I am called to walk in love, imitating His sacrificial love and extending grace to others. (Ephesians 5:1-2)

85. In Christ, I am empowered to live a life of purity and holiness, set apart for His purposes. (1 Thessalonians 4:7)

86. In Christ, I am an overcomer, conquering every trial and temptation through His strength. (Romans 8:37)

87. In Christ, I am called to walk in humility and gentleness, bearing with one another in love. (Ephesians 4:2)

88. In Christ, I am filled with His joy, rejoicing in His salvation and goodness. (Philippians 4:4)

89. In Christ, I am a vessel of His grace, filled with His Spirit and empowered to live for His glory. (2 Timothy 2:21)

90. In Christ, I am called to walk in obedience to His word, living a life that honors and pleases Him. (Colossians 3:16)

91. In Christ, I am called to be a witness of His love and truth, proclaiming His gospel to the ends of the earth. (Acts 1:8)

92. In Christ, I am called to walk in faith, trusting in His promises

and believing for His miracles. (Hebrews 11:6)

93. In Christ, I am strengthened with power through His Spirit, able to endure and persevere through all things. (Ephesians 3:16)

94. In Christ, I am called to walk in unity with fellow believers, bearing with one another in love. (Ephesians 4:3)

95. In Christ, I am a chosen people, a royal priesthood, a holy nation, God's special possession. (1 Peter 2:9)

96. In Christ, I am a co-heir with Christ, sharing in His inheritance

and glory. (Romans 8:17)

97. In Christ, I am called to bear fruit, producing a harvest of righteousness and love. (John 15:5)

98. In Christ, I am filled with the fruit of the Spirit, walking in love, joy, peace, patience, kindness, goodness, faithfulness, gentleness, and self-control. (Galatians 5:22-23)

99. In Christ, I am seated with Him in heavenly places, far above all

rule and authority, power and dominion. (Ephesians 1:20-21)

100. In Christ, I am redeemed and forgiven, set free from the power

of sin and death. (Ephesians 1:7

The kingdom of the air.

I don't know how many times my spirit went to the kingdom of the air. I have had out-of-body experiences, visions, and dreams about the kingdom of the air. The kingdom that Apostle Paul wrote about in Ephesians 6:12.

It is a kingdom, but a spiritual one—ruled by the prince of the air. The Devil is called the prince of the power of the air. You cannot dodge his influence if you are not in CHRIST. You have to be a serious and zealous believer if you are to be a warrior and a conqueror, and a student of the Word and spirit to defeat the powers of evil.

I have written articles, books, and eBooks explaining about the three heavens. The second heaven theory is not scriptural, however, as Apostle Paul was caught up in the Third heaven, in Paradise, logically we can assume that there is the first, second, and third. Some things we are going to need the person of the HOLY SPIRIT to reveal them to us.

The LORD GOD has been gracious to us by manifesting Himself unto us through dreams, visions, angels, through His word, and other means of communication. We cannot box the LORD in a container. His ways cannot be comprehended. As heaven is far above the earth, so are His ways.

In the second heaven, there are spirits, human spirits that are bound, some people are still on this earth. Strange fallen beings are holding in hostage the souls of men and humans. And when the times come, or when they die, their soul are already captured in the spirit realm to work for the kingdom of darkness.

A soul that is not covered by the blood of the lamb is bound by the powers of the air. On your own, you cannot defeat the evil influence of Satan in your waking life. You need the WORD, HOLY SPIRIT, and THE BLOOD.

The Devil is a soul snatcher, he looks at your generational DNA, if there is an open door of any kind, he will throw arrows until he brings you down. One of the greatest ignorance I have witnessed in those people bound, mostly it was due to sexual immorality, fornication, or abortion. Not to say these are great sins, but there is no small sin—sin is a sin.

In these last days, sexual sins have skyrocketed. Many fall because of sexual contact before marriage.

Marriages have collapsed. Leaders have fallen. Preachers, pastors, and prophets have lost dignity. The enemy is playing the chess game here.

These are the realm that cages the souls of men; the marine kingdom under the sea, the second heaven, and the kingdom underground. We can also include the occultist, witches, and wizards who cages the souls of men and women through their demonic powers.

Let's talk about the air realm. There is the first heaven, the second heaven, and the third heaven. The disembodied spirits are the evil spirits of the Nephilim destroyed during the floods of Noah.

Lucifer also fell with millions of angels. Apart from Lucifer, 200 watchers had sex with women—recorded in the book of Enoch and Genesis 6. The evil spirits hover around in the sky, looking for a way to a man. The sin of man gives this spirit legal authority to enter man's body.

It is to say, above our homes, in the air, there a thousands of evil spirits. Above the peak of the mountain, in the space of the clouds, there is a strongman who gives orders to these demons. Strongman is a serious power of authority. There are levels of degrees in the demonic. JESUS CHRIST granted us the power to cast out demons and also to bind strongmen.

The first heaven is where the powers of authority seats. They control what is going on in a region. But they have control only where they have legal rights. Satan can only control where there is a legal right to do so. He is limited.

The second heaven is his domain—headquarters. Where there are dangerous spirits like the queen of heaven, Ashtoreth, Jezebel, etc. this is the kingdom like any other kingdom. This is where the souls of men and women are caged. The real battle of spiritual warfare is here but with the angelic beings. This is where Angel Michael fought the Prince of Persia for the release of Gabriel to bring Daniel's message.

Principalities mostly name themselves according to the city of the domain they rule. If there was a principality in Johannesburg, he would call himself the prince of Johannesburg. However, these are fallen angels. You cannot cast them out. They are not demons but fallen angels. You can only restrict their assignment. You can be like Daniel and intercede for the dispatcher of angelic powers like Michael to fight for you when dealing with serious powers.

If you can picture yourself seated in the heavenly places with CHRIST, your faith will explode. Your level of spiritual perception will change. You start seeing yourself as above principalities and powers of darkness as you are seated in the seat of authority with CHRIST who has triumphed.

Colossians 1:15 Who is the image of the invisible God, the firstborn of every creature:

16 For by him were all things created, that are in heaven, and that are in

earth, visible and invisible, whether they be thrones, or dominions, or

principalities, or powers: all things were created by him, and for him: 17 And he

is before all things, and by him all things consist.

We are dealing with the invisible kingdoms that are pulling strings in the background. The naked eye cannot see spirits. Through the eyes of your mind—the Holy Spirit, you can see beyond time and space.

This few months I have been researching and writing about the discerning spirit (Spirit of discernment). This gift is important especially when dealing with spiritual attacks from the realm of darkness. It comes with words of wisdom, knowledge, and understanding of the spirit world.

Many times my life has been spared through this gift. And many has ago, I had a personal encounter with the LORD, and He was telling me about "intuition". Sometimes you will not get the word for a specific thing, or rather prophecy for a season when you need it most, if you can follow your intuition—your spirit within, you will succeed because the Holy Spirit is intertwined with our spirit, and bear witness to your heart.

This is also important when you are dealing with the marine powers. You will need the word for the moment. Your dream and vision life has to be covered by the power of the BLOOD OF JESUS. Marine powers works through dreams and visions. Sometimes they will confuse your life. Cover everything with the blood of the Cross. The power of GOD shall be revealed. Sing Holy Spirit-inspired songs—especially about the power of the BLOOD OF CHRIST.

Ephesians 1:19 And what is the exceeding greatness of his power to us-ward who

believe, according to the working of his mighty power,

20 Which he wrought in Christ, when he raised him from the dead, and set

him at his own right hand in the heavenly places,

CHRIST's priesthood is different from others, His priesthood is eternal. This means that you have been with CHRIST all along before you were even created, spiritually. The kingdom of GOD is spiritual. GOD is spiritual. JESUS CHRIST is a spirit being. However, He came in the bodily form for our redemption. The redemption plan of GOD has been ever since before creation. GOD knows the end from the beginning. Knows the thoughts of a man from afar.

In spirit, you are crafted in CHRIST who overcame. And that makes you an overcomer! Even though darkness has its way around us, we are the light of this world through CHRIST. Stir up your light! Arise and shine!

Ephesians 1:21 Far above all principality, and power, and might, and dominion, and

every name that is named, not only in this world, but also in that which is to

come:

IN THE WORLD TO COME CHRIST is still the KINGS! The wisdom of this world would try to convince you that Satan does not exist; it is all in your mind. The people in high power are those blinding many to believe the fallacy. Our enemy, the Devil sits at the seat of high authority in this world—manipulating, controlling, stealing, and killing.

A defeated foe indeed! But the media magnifies him to weaken man's faith. Our gateway through the presence of GOD is the Holy Spirit. the Holy Spirit in you is bigger than Satan a million times. The Holy Spirit is GOD. In other words, GOD resides in you. CHRIST in you is the hope of your glory. CHRIST in you is your salvation. No weapon formed against us shall prosper. It is the truth that shall set people free. In the name of the LORD GOD MOST HIGH be free!

GOD is above culture. GOD is above religion. GOD is above tradition. GOD is above all wisdom, all knowledge, and all understanding. Serve Him only in the name of JESUS CHRIST!

Ephesians 2:6 And hath raised us up together, and made us sit together in heavenly

places in Christ Jesus:

As we are in CHRIST, we have all the spiritual blessings to free ourselves and our brethren from spiritual bondage of all kinds. The Psalmist says we are a little lower than the angels. This is great authority indeed. What's more? Psalm 82:6 *"Ye are gods"*. We all come from the HOLY ONE!

Psalm 82:6 I have said, Ye are gods; and all of you are children of the most High.

In dealing with the demonic realm like the marine kingdom, a very basic strategy of success in war is to know one's enemy. Without exception, a general would never take his army against another army without first preparing the soldiers.

Foundational to that preparation would be a study of the strengths and weaknesses of the enemy. Failure to study the enemy would virtually guarantee defeat— even if the opposing army were inferior. Throughout this book, I talk in depth about who our enemy is, you will be surprised that even though this book is about the marine battle, most focus is on the Devil himself and overcoming strategies of victory against his tricks.

Most of my writing is in line of spiritual warfare and prayer mainly because we are in war. The battle is for the LORD but He uses us as His mighty army to dismantle the powers of darkness throughout the world. People must be free from demonic entanglement. There is freedom in the LORD.

CHRIST has to be known from sun rising to sun down. This is the greatest commission of the gospel.

Psalm 34: 8 O taste and see that the LORD is good: blessed is the man that trusteth in

him.

Marine kingdom cages.

We have already talked about the second heaven territory. We as the body of CHRIST are endowed from above by the MOST HIGH in CHRIST. We are seated in the heavenly places spiritually. We fight from a heavenly perspective. And we fight the good fight of faith.

Marine cages are prison cells where they keep the souls of men and women. The kingdom under the sea is responsible for many atrocious activities happening in the world and in the body of CHRIST.

CHRIST is raising the generation of believers who will not only be limited by time and space, but wherever the spirit leads them, they will go. As Philip was time traveling through the spirit of GOD, his end-time armies shall work the kingdom business in the spirit realm, taking territories and demolishing the works of the Evil one. In the spirit, the realm is about power and authority. It is about territories and the powers of the Words.

The kingdom of CHRIST is the kingdom of power demonstrated by the words of power through the HOLY SPIRIT. When you have the Word and spirit of CHRIST, you can shake the nations.

Sadly, many do have them but practice only one. Many read the Word staunchly, however, fail to invite the person of the HOLY SPIRIT to take over. In the beginning, GOD spoke and commanded, and it was established, the heavens and the earth. He spoke the Word, and the HOLY SPIRIT acted upon the Word. We are to speak the Word in every situation we may encounter, it is the HOLY SPIRIT that shall act upon the Word. Even in the ministry of Angels, angels act only upon the Word of GOD.

As CHRIST led the captivity after His death, we are to practice deliverance. Lead our friends and family out of the land of destruction. Out of the pit of hell. There are many spirits of the people on this earth that are in hell already while still living. I have seen many souls caged in the second heaven, under the sea, in the mountains, etc. By the way, mountains, and seas are portals to the other side of the world. Many rituals in this world are either done in the mountains or the seas.

As I write to you reader, you may be having friends and family members who are in bondage. We do not have to fear; CHRIST is the bondage breaker. The Devil is already defeated but he does not want you to know it. we already know that his kingdom is built upon fear, lies, manipulation, and deception. He rebelled to GOD. He wants you to rebel also.

In the next chapters, I will include a deliverance plan for freedom. And fire prayers which are scriptural to defeat the powers of hell. Do not allow hell to enlarge itself upon your life and your family. The recipe and the remedy is to fight the good fight of faith. Fight through righteousness. Fight through faith. Fight through peace. Fight through with all kinds of prayers. Sing in spirit like King David. Be mighty with the sword (Word of GOD) like Joshua. DELIVERANCE AND BLESSINGS COME FROM THE LORD (PSALM 3:9).

Binding and loosing.

The principle of binding and loosing is a deliverance tool to restrict the powers of darkness and banish them from your life. When the enemy comes, he comes to steal, kill, and destroy. He steals first before he can kill and destroy. We have the power to spoil what he has stolen from us. You can bind him and lose whatsoever he has spoiled you.

CHRIST defeated principalities and spoiled them. We see the same principle when the Israelites were coming out of Egypt, they defeated Pharaoh and spoiled his nation. They came out of slavery rich.

Your deliverance must bear a change in your life. When you are delivered from empty pockets you go from empty pockets to full pockets. From poverty to rich. From unbelief to faith. From weak faith to strong faith. You move from point A to point B. This is the principle of deliverance.

Looking at the principle of binding and losing, Satan rules from the mid-heavens over a well-organized army. He divides the earth into principalities ruled over by princes, also called strongmen. The strongmen sit on thrones in the mid-heavens and rule over the evil spirits on earth. They give orders and strength to the spirits under their command.

So, sometimes to cast these spirits, you will have to bind the strongman before you cast them out. There are weak spirits and strong ones. Strong demons are those that take time to come out of a person. But they can through prayer and fasting. Jesus spoke on this in Mathew 17:21 that some demons won't be expelled except through fasting.

With all kinds of prayer, we should minister unto the LORD.

Unless we bind up the strongmen, it is difficult to cast out demons. In Matthew 16:19, Jesus instructs us to bind up the strongman. He repeats his admonition in Mark 3:27 and warns us in Matthew 12:29 that we cannot spoil the strongman's house unless we first bind up the strongman: *"Or else how can one enter into a strong man's house, and spoil his goods, except he first bind the strongman? and then he will spoil his house."*

The children of Israel defeated Pharaoh and spoiled the nation of Egypt. They came out of Egypt wealthy. Pharaoh was a strongman—represented the gods and goddesses of Egypt—a principality. You bind the strongman before you can spoil him.

You can self-deliver yourself. This book is full of do it yourself. I personally, deliver myself from time to time. If you have faith in the Word and in prayer, deliverance comes naturally. It is an act of deliverance to meditate on the Word. It is an act of deliverance to sing Psalms, Hymns, and spiritual songs in spirit and truth.

Many times I have seen great breakthroughs by just singing songs about the blood of JESUS. Command demons in your life to come out. Bind the prince of the power of the air—silence his influence on your life. Cover your territory with blood prayer. You will see light.

The church badly needs to learn how to bind the enemy both here on earth and in the heavenlies. The fight is in the spirit realm, so we act by faith in the Word of God. We cannot see the strongman, but we know its works.

For we wrestle not against flesh and blood, but against principalities, against powers, against the rulers of the darkness of this world, against spiritual wickedness in high places. (Eph. 6:12)

"Rulers of the darkness of this world" and *"spiritual wickedness in high places"* refer to strongmen.

And I give unto thee the keys of the kingdom of heaven: and whatsoever thou shalt bind on earth shall be bound in heaven: and whatsoever thou shalt loose on earth shall be loosed in heaven. (Matt. 16:19)

Again, in Matthew 18:18, He says:

Verily I say unto you, Whatsoever ye shall bind on earth shall be bound in heaven: and whatsoever ye shall loose on earth shall be loosed in heaven.

Child of God, we need to wake up and realize that we have been given much more authority than we have ever imagined! It is no longer a matter of prayer by which we cry out, Oh, God, please come and do something about this awful devil that is giving me such a hard time." But it is a matter of rising in the power of the name of Jesus and telling the devil what he has to do!!

Child of God, the victory over Satan and demonic attacks has already been won by Jesus. As far as heaven is concerned every captive is loosed! The principle is the same in salvation. Jesus has provided for every man's salvation. But, why are people still lost? The blood must be applied by every man. Every man who, by faith, applies the blood of Jesus Christ to his life is saved. Those who refuse or neglect to receive Jesus Christ as their personal Savior will be eternally lost. In like manner, those who refuse or neglect to accept their birthright of deliverance will be bound in this life.

The Word of GOD

The only piece of the spiritual warrior's armor that is both offensive and defensive is named last on Paul's list: "the sword of the Spirit, which is the word of God" (Ephesians 6:17). William Gurnall aptly describes this piece of armor:

The sword is the weapon continually used by soldiers to defend themselves and to rout their enemies. Thus it illustrates the most excellent use of God's Word, by which the believer both defends himself and cuts down his enemies.... Because Satan is a spirit we must fight him with spiritual arms. And the Word is a spiritual sword.... God's army overcomes every enemy by one of two ways—conversion or destruction. The Word of God is the sword which affects both—it has two edges. This two-edged sword is the very weapon Jesus used to withstand Satan in the wilderness. Jesus had studied Scripture from His boyhood and filled His mind with its truth. Thus, in the moment of crisis, His sword was sharp and ready. All it took to defeat the enemy was "every word that comes from the mouth of the LORD"

(Deuteronomy 8:3).

Hebrews 4:12 particularly speaks of the power of the Word: "For the word of God is living and active. Sharper than any double-edged sword, it penetrates even to dividing soul and spirit, joints and marrow; it judges the thoughts and attitudes of the heart."

The Word is the power force of GOD. The Word changes everything. The Word is power. The Word is glorious. The Word of GOD does not fail. The Word sent forth shall accomplish what the LORD GOD wishes to accomplish. Stand on the ground of the mighty Word of GOD. Taste and see the goodness of the Word of GOD. Take the Word by faith—birth dreams, visions, and promises of GOD in your waking life.

On your deliverance from captivity, you stand in the Word. If it is written, believe it, it shall come to pass. "I speak, therefore, I believe". You can only speak if you believe. He has magnified His Word above His name. that's how much the Word is to be valued and upheld.

Psalm 138:2 I will worship toward thy holy temple, and praise thy name for thy

lovingkindness and for thy truth: for thou hast magnified thy word above all thy

name.

This scripture shows us the greatest weapon of all time—the Word. It has been magnified above the names of GOD. We know that the names of GOD are holy and powerful. But here the scripture speaks otherwise, about the power of the Word. The Word is the person of JESUS CHRIST. He has been exalted above all. He is your ticket to your salvation, in this time, and in the ages to come. CHRIST is your KING!

Scriptures

Then the LORD said to Moses, "Write down these words, for in accordance with these words I have made a covenant with you and with Israel" (Exodus 34:27).

If anyone does not listen to my words that the prophet speaks in my name, I myself will call him to account (Deuteronomy 18:19).

Take to heart all the words I have solemnly declared to you this day, so that you may command your children to obey carefully all the words of this law. They are not just idle words for you— they are your life (Deuteronomy 32:46-47).

When the king heard the words of the Book of the Law, he tore his robes.... "Go and inquire of the LORD for me and for the people and for all Judah about what is written in this book that has been found. Great is the LORD'S anger that burns against us because our fathers have not obeyed the words of this book" (2 Kings 22:11-13).

They mocked God's messengers, despised his words and scoffed at his prophets until the wrath of the LORD was aroused against his people and there was no remedy (2 Chronicles 36:16).

My soul faints with longing for your salvation, but I have put my hope in your word.... Your word is a lamp to my feet and a light for my path.... Your statutes are my heritage forever; they are the joy of my heart. My heart is set on keeping your decrees to the very end (Psalm 119:81,105,111-12).

The unfolding of your words gives light; it gives understanding to the simple.... All your words are true; all your righteous laws are eternal (Psalm 119:130,160).

I will bow down toward your holy temple and will praise your name for your love and your faithfulness, for you have exalted above all things your name and your word (Psalm 138:2).

I [God] make known the end from the beginning, from ancient times, what is still to come. I say: My purpose will stand, and I will do all that I please.... What I have said, that will I bring about; what I have planned, that will I do (Isaiah 46:10-11).

So is my word that goes out from my mouth: It will not return to me empty, but will accomplish what I desire and achieve the

purpose for which I sent it (Isaiah 55:11).

"Is not my word like fire," declares the LORD, "and like a

hammer that breaks a rock in pieces?" (Jeremiah 23:29).

The LORD has done what he planned; he has fulfilled his word,

which he decreed long ago.... Who can speak and have it happen

if the Lord has not decreed it? (Lamentations 2:17; 3:37).

You must speak my words to them, whether they listen or fail to

listen, for they are rebellious.... "None of my words will be

delayed any longer; whatever I say will be fulfilled, declares the

Sovereign LORD" (Ezekiel 2:7; 12:28).

By your words you will be acquitted, and by your words you

will be condemned (Matthew 12:37).

Heaven and earth will pass away, but my words will never pass

away (Matthew 24:35).

For with God nothing is ever impossible and no word from God

shall be without power or impossible of fulfillment (Luke 1:37,

AMP).

In the beginning was the Word, and the Word was with God, and the Word was God.... In him was life, and that life was the light of men (John 1:1,4).

I tell you the truth, whoever hears my word and believes him who sent me has eternal life and will not be condemned; he has crossed over from death to life.... If anyone keeps my word, he will never see death (John 5:24; 8:51).

"The Spirit gives life; the flesh counts for nothing. The words I have spoken to you are spirit and they are life...." Simon Peter answered him, "Lord, to whom shall we go? You have the words of eternal life" (John 6:63,68).

Faith comes from hearing the message, and the message is heard through the word of Christ (Romans 10:17).

God's word is not chained (2 Timothy 2:9).

For you have been born again, not of perishable seed, but of imperishable, through the living and enduring word of God. For, "... the grass withers and the flowers fall, but the word of the Lord stands forever." And this is the word that was preached to you (1 Peter 1:23-25).

The word of God lives in you, and you have overcome the evil one (1 John 2:14).

These are the words of him who has the sharp, double-edged sword.... Repent therefore! Otherwise, I will soon come to you and will fight against them with the sword of my mouth (Revelation 2:12,16).

He who was seated on the throne said, "I am making everything new!" Then he said, "Write this down, for these words are trustworthy and true" (Revelation 21:5).

Prayer

Lord, I rejoice that the sword of the Spirit—the Word of God, our chief weapon—helps me to pray both defensively and offensively. Thank You, Jesus, for setting an example for us when You declared Scripture to defeat Satan in the wilderness. Teach me to wield this Sword of the Spirit with power in my prayers so that I may have victory over the enemy. In Your name, amen.

The Blood of the Lamb

———

Blood prayer sets the captives free. The tiny drop of the blood of CHRIST will silence matters in the kingdom of darkness. The is nothing powerful than the blood of JESUS CHRIST. As you are dealing with an ancestral stronghold, curses, marine powers, and a strongman of evil in your life, the blood is potent to set you free in an instant. For me, this came through a revelation. The LORD revealed the power of His blood.

Just by singing blood songs such as "Awesome Blood" and "Nothing but the Blood" you can be delivered from any satanic stronghold. However, it all comes down to faith. You have to believe that what you are praying for shall surely come to pass.

You can cover your home with the blood of JESUS just like Moses who ordered the Israelites in Egypt to put the blood in their doorpost. Whoever did put the blood of the lamb on their doorpost was spared from death. The blood of JESUS delivers you from the grip of death. Death no longer has power over you. Death is a spirit. Death is our enemy. When do not die but sleep in the LORD and rise in the LORD. Heaven is our ultimate home.

The Angel of Death destroyed the firstborn of Egypt, including Pharaoh's son who was about to precede him. A man who has not made a blood covenant with CHRIST will always be in Egypt. Egypt is the house of bondage. The yoke of bondage will be heavy on you. Deliverance comes from the house of the LORD.

Exodus 12:12 For I will pass through the land of Egypt this night, and will smite all the

firstborn in the land of Egypt, both man and beast; and against all the gods of

Egypt I will execute judgment: I am the LORD.

13 And the blood shall be to you for a token upon the houses where ye are:

and when I see the blood, I will pass over you, and the plague shall not be upon

you to destroy you, when I smite the land of Egypt.

The blood of Jesus is one of the potent weapons against spiritual wickedness in high places and to demolish every stronghold of satanic forces. It cannot achieve less for you.

Revelation 12:11: *"And they overcame him by the blood of the Lamb and the Word of their testimony and they loved not their lives unto the death."*

The blood of Jesus can never lose its power because it is a divine blood. Jesus is the only begotten of the father" (John 1:14). The blood of Jesus avails for everything imaginable. If we are going to experience the power in the blood of Jesus we have to personally apply it to our lives and our situations. We apply the blood of Jesus, by decrees, *i.e.* we confess it.

The blood of Jesus speaks better things than the blood of Abel" (Hebrews 12:24). The blood of Jesus can speak destruction upon your enemies, healing to your body, protection to your family, *etc.* The blood of Jesus brings life to you. The Bible says, "The life of the flesh is in the blood: . . ."(Leviticus 17:11). The blood of Jesus contains the life of Jesus. Divine life! The power for overcoming is in this blood.

Exodus 5:1 And afterward Moses and Aaron went in, and told Pharaoh, Thus saith the

LORD God of Israel, Let my people go, that they may hold a feast unto me in the wilderness.

It was after the blood that Pharaoh left them. Every pharaoh that does want to leave you is about to leave by the power of the blood of the lamb. Exodus 12 chapter shows us the power of the blood of the lamb. JESUS is still as powerful today to deliver you from every marine power. Even if Pharaoh pursues you, the arm of the LORD is so strong that it overthrows the horse and its riders. No weapon shall destroy you.

Exodus 11:4 And Moses said, Thus saith the LORD, About midnight will I go out into

the midst of Egypt:

AMAZINGLY, PASSOVER happened in Exodus chapter 12. And again, the LORD about midnight went before them. Midnight is 12 too. 12 is a special number to GOD. JESUS walked with 12 Apostles. There are 12 tribes of Israel. 12 gates in the third heaven. 12 doors whereby the names of the Apostles are written. Apostle

Peter couldn't continue in ministry before they found an Apostle to fill the space of Judas Iscariot. 12 is the number of completions.

At the end of this book, I will include blood prayer for destroying demonic powers. We plead the blood, speak the blood scriptures, and apply it to situations to change. You may be seeking deliverance from stagnation, poverty, or demonic ties of ancestral powers, the blood can deliver you.

Ministry of Angels.

———

My encounter with Michael.

Let me start by saying, I grew up in a South African village called Mashashane. It is one of the most feared villages in the region for witchcraft. If you ever travel to South Africa, you will hear about the province where I am from as the cornerstone of witchcraft practices. Anyway, witchcraft is widespread in Africa and beyond. So as a Christian believer, my view of how the enemy operates with always be different from the Western belief.

Because where I am from we do not hear about witchcraft but see it with our own eyes. The village has molded me into being the prayer warrior I am today. You will always see the emphasis on prayer in my writing. Especially spiritual warfare, which I believe many are starting to be woken to the reality that life is spiritual.

From an early age, my eyes have always been opened to the spiritual world. I used to see angels, demons, and agents of the Devil in spirit even before I became a staunch believer. Parents always stressed prayer before sleep. My grandmother when she was around—would call me at midnight to pray. She always knew that this was the time when witches and wizards met to perform their demonic assignments.

Not that we were leaving in fear of the Devil, no. men and women ought to meet with GOD in their secret place as they commit and devotion to their GOD. It started with prayer then we started fasting, and reading the Word of GOD. This is the roadmap of a serious spiritual journey. He says come with thanksgiving and praise in my court.

The gates of GOD open when we offer thanksgiving. But the journey does not stop there. We get to the courtroom of GOD through praise.

Psalm 100: 4 Enter into his gates with thanksgiving, and into his courts with praise: be thankful unto him, and bless his name.

This verse has been the pillar of my life. I knew that this verse entails the gateway to the heart of GOD. The gateway to the glory of GOD. David was a man after GOD's heart because he placed the act of praise above all things. What you worship and what you praise control you. The spirit of GOD was at move-in David. Even after he committed adultery and murder, he pleaded with GOD to not remove the Holy Spirit from him and upon him.

There are two places where you find the term 'Holy Spirit' in the Old Testament. In Psalm 51:11 and Isaiah 63:10. Although there are different instances of the works of the holy spirit. Here I am referring to the term "Holy Spirit" which is popularly known in the New Testament, especially in the Acts of Apostles.

The reason why I am emphasizing prayer, fasting, praise, and worship is that these principles of the kingdom have opened my eyes to the spirit world where you meet celestial bodies and the divine. JESUS CHRIST speaks at all times, whether we hear or miss it, He speaks. I have met him through a series of dreams and visions. I am in the prophetic office by the call of GOD, as a prophetic it is vital to be sensitive to the spirit of the world.

This is where the spirit of discerning comes in. To be able to discern between good and evil. The renewed mind of CHRIST will always know the perfect will of GOD. There are some brothers and sisters who were fooled by the Angels of the Devil masquerading as the Angels of Light. I don't know anyone who has ever met a horned-red Devil in dreams or visions.

The enemy will appear pleasing. You will always see this beautiful mermaid televised in Hollywood. The world will make Satan look innocent and make GOD evil. This is the generation that celebrates evil as Holy and Holy as evil. We have come to that. So, brothers and sisters, the enemy will not trick you or manipulate you if it looks phony and ugly.

Satan is the most handsome dude ever. Almost all fallen and demons shapeshift to glorious state when they want to deceive the world. Therefore, do not neglect the free spiritual gifts Christ has died for on the Cross. We are spiritually blessed in High places in CHRIST. Note that, these evil powers also have strongholds in high places. But you are far above them because CHRIST dwells in the highest of the heavens to date, which is the third heaven.

Ephesians 1:21 Far above all principality, and power, and might, and dominion, and every name that is named, not only in this world, but also in that which is to come:

We meet Angelic powers like Michael and Gabriel because we are in CHRIST. Even Moses the great man of GOD, saw JESUS CHRIST in spirit. I received the revelation that all prophets of GOD in the bible had an encounter with the FATHER and

CHRIST. Adam as the first man, it would be revealed that there will be a second Adam.

It was GOD in the Garden of Eden who clothed Adam and Eve after deception. The blood of the Animal was from Lambs. The blood of the Lamb was shed in the garden. The Garden of Eden is the face of GOD. It means that to meet GOD, you have to go through the process of Blood. Abraham also, after Mount Moriah's sacrifice, went on to have a deeper relationship with GOD like never before.

There is power in the blood of the Lamb. All the Angels of GOD point us to a deeper relationship with the GOD of the universe. Any Angel that doesn't lead you to Almighty GOD is a false one. Michael the prince, is the warrior commander of the Heavenly Armies under the leadership of GOD and CHRIST. All Angels listen and perform the Word of GOD.

Psalm 105:20 Bless the LORD, ye his angels, that excel in strength, that do his commandments, hearkening unto the voice of his word.

Angels are very powerful. You cannot retain strength if one of them walks into your room right now. Angels were created from fire. They are ministers of fire. Even swords they carry flames with the fire of the glory of GOD. What's more, they live in the presence of GOD which is fiery.

I always do wage warfare for my village—pleading the blood of JESUS over my community and interceding on behalf of my people to come to CHRIST. I did not know that all along Angel Michal was dispatched to assist me over my community. In spirit, I will see the bright clouds over my community after spiritual warfare. I would see principal demons and fallen ones leave the area after an intense battle. Bear in mind that, this is a once-off thing.

Many would say it is not scriptural to wage warfare in the heavenly. If you are a strategic prophet, you will see the need to wage good warfare for your community or city as Prophet Daniel did. Prophet Daniel through territorial warfare was able to foster and change the future of Israel. Knowing the truth will make us stand on the truth. When he learned from the book of Jeremiah the Prophet that it would take 70 years of captivity, he went to his knees and reasoned with the Most High.

He was allowed to see the future Messiah and the end of the world. I believe some of the information he was not allowed to share. It was information sealed for the wise. Every now and then, men and women must stand up in their faith to wage warfare for their community because this is what the agents of Satan do. They fight for the territory of cities, towns, and villages, they occupy these regions if Christians are not in prayer and unity in faith.

For every territorial warfare, Archangel Michael arises. Where there is Prince of Persia, Michael is there. Where there is Satan, Michael is there. Michael is the prince over believers and over those who fear the LORD. The fear of the LORD is the beginning of all beautiful things. All things come from the sincere reverend of the Mighty King.

Hebrews 1:14 Are they not all ministering spirits, sent forth to minister for them who shall be heirs of salvation?

He gives Angels charge over us, to protect us and defend us against the wiles of the enemy.

Psalm 34: 7 The angel of the LORD encampeth round about them that fear him, and delivereth them.

Psalm 35: 5 Let them be as chaff before the wind: and let the angel of the LORD chase them.

Psalm 91: 11 For he shall give his angels charge over thee, to keep thee in all thy ways. 12 They shall bear thee up in their hands, lest thou dash thy foot against a stone.

Satan quoted this line while tempting JESUS. Throughout history, people of faith have been using Psalms 91 as their protective charm against the wiles of the Devil. For Satan to quote it, it means it's a powerful protective Psalm. I have seen the power of GOD while using this Psalm, meditating on it, praying on it, and acting on it. JESUS CHRIST is the secret place of the MOST HIGH. He is the highest priest in the kingdom of GOD who opened the veil of His body so that we can experience the Divine presence of the MOST HIGH GOD.

In the book of Ephesians 2:6, we are seated with CHRIST in the heavenly places. We all know that JESUS CHRIST is in paradise in the 3rd heaven. The secret place is a spiritual place not a physical place. It is in CHRIST who is seated in the right hand of the Mighty Father. This is the place of POWER. Man and women of GOD draw powers and authority from this glorified place of light.

The moment of writing this piece, I went outside to relieve myself. In villages we have outside toilets unlike in towns. As I came outside, I saw the Host of heaven (Angels) moving in a different direction in the sky. My eyes were open in spirit to see this beautiful vision. I believe it was a confirmation for me to continue writing this book.

Because I always had that desire and sensation to write a book about Angels since many do not have deep knowledge of these celestial bodies. I had only a few encounters that I could include, but would not make a full print. I did a thorough research, then I stopped.

A thing about me, I write when I am inspired by the Spirit of GOD. Today I am truly inspired to write this piece of work to you.

Okay, my encounter with Michael happened in spirit, in spirit I mean an out-of-body experience where I felt like I was fighting demons in the sky over my region but outer space. There a kingdoms and governments of evil forces in the heavenly places. Apostle Paul wrote about these powers in Ephesians 6:12—principalities and powers of evil.

To really establish the government of GOD in your home or city, you have to go the extra mile. Destined people are separated from the world. You would have to be separated like Elijah and John the Baptist. You can receive serious divine revelation and knowledge when you are in the wilderness alone. Sadly, many do not want to take the narrow road. The narrow road is the way to home.

Looking at prophets and Apostles in the bible, they had a distinct lifestyle of prayer. They were into the ministry of the Word and Prayer. By prayer, I mean all kinds of prayers. As we are advised to pray all kinds of prayers in the book of Ephesians.

Every human being has a guardian angel from birth. However, those called by GOD have special armies waiting to lead them into their destiny. There are different kinds of angels with different tasks. Michael is widely known for defending the people of Israel and believers in general from all walks of life. Prophets and Apostles mostly encounter this angelic force since He is a spiritual warfare warrior.

When Michael arises, there comes victory. He never loses a battle. He demoted Lucifer from heaven. He will still be in future chains and throw him in the eternal damnation reserved for fallen angels as it is written about him.

Revelation 20: 1-2 And I saw an angel come down from heaven, having the key of the bottomless pit and a great chain in his hand. 2 And he laid hold on the dragon, that old serpent, which is the Devil, and Satan, and bound him a thousand years,

The prophetic army of GOD its defender is Angel Michael and His angels. He was with Moses in Egypt. And led him to victory. He was with Samuel, Gideon, Barak, David, Jehoshaphat, Apostles, and more.

Even today, He is still with us. Fighting principalities and powers warring with believers each day. When Archangel Michael is around fear goes, and peace reigns. When you are propelled to decree and declare in spirit, know that the angels are around.

I have had a deep experience with Michael during my warfare seasons with evil forces and powers of the sky. There is a level that one reaches when all hell has been tempering with your destiny in your life. Those who go through rough seasons in life are destined for greatness. We are all destined for greatness. But they are those with special assignments like the caliber of Elijah, John the Baptist, Jeremiah, JESUS CHRIST, etc.

I believe you are also one of the special warriors for the end time season to wage war on the kingdom of darkness through your faith. Faith is paramount. Faith is the key. Faith is everything. Keep the faith and keep going till the end of time. No weapon formed against you shall prosper. It's only a matter of time before you shall be elevated and mount up with wings and fly.

There a horses of fire in heaven waiting for you. These are the horses of the end-time warfare. Where at that day CHRIST will be the king from sea to sea, border to border, from the sun rising to the sun going down. For years I have been seeing this vision—horses riding swiftly coming through the white clouds—Christ wearing the crown, red apparel followed by tenths of thousands of holy ones.

Revelation 19:11 And I saw heaven opened, and behold a white horse; and he that sat upon him was called Faithful and True, and in righteousness he doth judge and make war. 12 His eyes were as a flame of fire, and on his head were many crowns; and he had a name written, that no man knew, but he himself. 13 And he was clothed with a vesture dipped in blood: and his name is called The Word of God. 14 And the armies which were in heaven followed him upon white horses, clothed in fine linen, white and clean. 15 And out of his mouth goeth a sharp sword, that with it he should smite the nations: and he shall rule them with a rod of iron: and he treadeth the winepress of the fierceness and wrath of Almighty God. 16 And he

I always say the time we are in are the most important timeline in history. All the prophecy of the ancient biblical prophet's point to these days. As it was in the days of Noah, so shall it be in our days. Even though we do not know the day or the hour, but signs speaks loud. It is a set time to walk in the spirit of GOD. To exercise walking in faith more and more. GOD bless.

High Praises and Two edged sword.

―――

Psalm 149:5-9 Let the saints be joyful in glory: let them sing aloud upon their beds.

6 Let the high praises of God be in their mouth, and a twoedged sword in

their hand;

7 To execute vengeance upon the heathen, and punishments upon the

people;

8 To bind their kings with chains, and their nobles with fetters of iron;

9 To execute upon them the judgment written: this honour have all his

saints. Praise ye the LORD.

We fight for our freedom. Praise song has been the pillar for deliverance in my instances. Throughout history, through Psalms and Hymns, believers have tamed the powers of darkness. Apostle Paul and Silas also did the same thing while imprisoned, they sang unto the LORD and got their deliverance breakthrough.

Scriptures say that GOD is spirit and looking for those who shall worship in spirit and truth. Therefore, our singing, worship, and praise should be sincere. We should mean business when we are contending with the powers of darkness. Many are grappling in darkness; witchcraft powers have robbed many lives.

The Word of GOD is the ultimate source of the songs of deliverance. When you really want to sing for the LORD, open His book, and sing His word. His Word is His will. His Word is His mind. By all means, we should try to mirror the Word into our lives.

Where I am from, I have seen many losing their lives after buying their first car, after their marriage, and after getting the dream job, many had been the victim of the evil powers at work. Spirit of Jealousy, murder, and witchcraft are at play most of the time.

When we get into spiritual warfare, we are taming those unseen forces of evil that want to swallow us. Because each and every day there are arrows of evil that fly. The sun and the moon shall not smite you when you live under the banner of the blood of Jesus.

We all have been the victim of circumstance, whether you believe it or not, there comes a time when you will say "Enough is enough". It will be a time of war. War with the principalities and powers of evil is scriptural, and it is real. There is a whole dimensions and kingdoms that are fighting humankind in general whereby the agents are rewarded for their evil deeds. It's a war between light and darkness.

Let the high praises of God be in their mouth, and a twoedged sword in

their hand;

High praises are warfare songs that shift the atmosphere. In the spirit, praises are like rising smoke going into the sky. The demons cannot stand the fire of the praise. Praise does not only shake the earth but the heavens as well. The two-edged sword is the Word of GOD.

Hebrews 4:12 For the word of God is quick, and powerful, and sharper than any

two-edged sword, piercing even to the dividing asunder of soul and spirit, and of

the joints and marrow, and is a discerner of the thoughts and intents of the heart.

The Word is the sword of the spirit we fight with. A soldier has the gadgets of war, a soldier in CHRIST has the weapon of spirit. These cannot be seen with naked eyes but with spiritual eyes. Spirituality rules and governs over the natural realm. We pray with understanding knowing that we possess potent weapons that can bring destruction to the kingdom of darkness.

2 Corinthians 10:3 For though we walk in the flesh, we do not war after the flesh:

4 (For the weapons of our warfare are not carnal, but mighty through God to

the pulling down of strong holds;)

5 Casting down imaginations, and every high thing that exalteth itself people are either influenced by the HOLY SPIRIT or the demons. You cannot be in between. Yes, as a Christian believer, demons may oppress, harass, and turn your life into a living hell if you open the door for them. It is all about law in the spirit realm. The whole concept of curt comes into play when these two kingdoms clash, which are the kingdom of darkness and the kingdom of light. Thus, CHRIST is our advocate. The Devil is a legalist –opposing us before the LIVING GOD about our sinful nature. In nature, man is sinful, we are only the new creature when we come to CHRIST and lay it all on His feet.

JESUS CHRIST is the feet of righteousness and holiness. Your only ticket to salvation. It is my wish that many could see salvation while in this life. The next life, it's a new chapter of eternal bliss or eternal corruption according to whom you served while in the land of the living.

We have mighty weapons through GOD to pull down strongholds. These mighty weapons are the reckoning force of deliverance. Deliverance comes from the LORD.

To bind their kings with chains, and their nobles with fetters of iron;

Through this power of praise, some of you will bind the king and queen in spirit—overthrowing the powers of the air that have been influencing your territory. You are seated in the heavenly places, in a place of authority to be above the kingdom of darkness. This authority and power comes from CHRIST. If CHRIST has given you power, it is clear that the kingdom of darkness has power as well.

As they always say, Satan has power but no authority. We can look at this from the story of Job. Satan couldn't do anything except if GOD allowed Him to. Through doing self-introspection of your own life, if there is any area where you are not walking in authority, the powers of darkness may be at work in that area. We are called to be above and not beneath, leaders not followers, and lenders not borrowers. This is what the word of GOD says about you.

WARFARE PRAYERS

Prayer is not only communion with God; it is confrontation with the enemy. These prayers are very helpful in spiritual warfare.

Put on the full armor of God so that you can take your stand against the devil's schemes. For our struggle is not against flesh and blood, but against the rulers, against the authorities, against the powers of this dark world and against the spiritual forces of evil in the heavenly realms. Therefore put on the full armor of God, so that when the day of evil comes, you may be able to stand your ground, and after you have done everything, to stand. Stand firm then with the belt of truth buckled around your waist, with the breastplate of righteousness in place, and with your feet fitted with the readiness that comes from the Gospel of peace. In addition to all this, take up the shield of faith, with which you can extinguish all the flaming arrows of the evil one. Take the helmet of salvation and the sword of the

THE ARMOR OF GOD

(based on Ephesians 6:13-17)

"Thank You, Lord, for my salvation. I receive it in a new and fresh way from You and I declare that nothing can separate me from the love of Christ and the place I have in Your kingdom. I wear Your righteousness today against all condemnation and corruption. Cover me with Your holiness and purity—defend me from all assaults against my heart. Lord, I put on the belt of truth. I choose a lifestyle of honesty and integrity. Expose the lies I have believed, and show me the truths I need today. I choose to live for the Gospel in every moment. Show me where You are working and lead me to it. Give me strength to walk daily with You. I believe that You are powerful against every lie and assault of the enemy. You have good in store for me. Nothing is coming today that can overcome me because You are with me. Holy Spirit, show

me the truths of the Word of God that I will need to counter the traps of the enemy. Bring those Scriptures to mind today. Finally, Holy Spirit, I agree to walk in step with You in everything as my spirit communes with You in prayer throughout the day."

THE WEAPONS OF WARFARE

(based on 2 Corinthians 10:4-5)

"Father, Your Word says that no weapon formed against me shall prosper (Isaiah 54:17). Therefore I declare that no weapon formed against me prospers this day or any day to come in Jesus' name. Your Word says that trouble will not arise a second time (Nahum 1:9). Therefore I declare that Satan cannot make trouble for me again, in this manner, as he did in the past in Jesus' name. I declare all of these prayers accomplished and brought to pass by trusting you through faith and expectation in the name of Jesus.

Lord Jesus, I confess to You all of my sins this day, yesterday and every day past. I repent and renounce them, those known and unknown, those of omission and commission, in what I have done and in what I have failed to do. I lay down at Your feet all of the sins of the flesh, the tongue, and of the heart, and all unholy thoughts and actions. Thank You, Lord, for shedding Your precious blood for me.

I stand on Your Word. The enemy is driven out from before me, above me, around me, and below me; from my home, workplace, church and its ministries, children, and loved ones; from my works and labors, land, and my presence. I declare that he is not able to stand against me, and his works are taken captive and destroyed. No weapon formed against me will prosper, for the Spirit of the Lord shall raise a standard against them. I declare all of these things accomplished by Your Word. Jesus, my Lord, I give You thanksgiving, praise, glory, honor and worship for Your righteousness and holiness given to me by Your Word on my behalf."

PROTECTION PRAYER

(based on 2 Corinthians 6:14-7:1, 10:3-5; Romans 12:1-2)

"Heavenly Father, I bow in worship and praise before You. I cover myself with the blood of the Lord Jesus Christ as my protection.

I surrender myself completely and unreservedly in every area of my life to You. I submit myself only to the true and living God and refuse any involvement of the enemy in my life. I choose to be transformed by the renewing of my mind. I pull down every thought that exalts itself against the knowledge of Christ. I pray and thank you for a sound mind, the mind of Christ.

Today and every day I ask for protection over my spouse; each of my children; our immediate family members, relatives, friends, acquaintances and myself. I also ask today for protection during all of our travels; for our provision, finances, possessions, health, safety, and welfare. I put all of these things under the covering of Your precious blood and declare that Satan cannot touch them, on this day or any day to come."

GENERAL CONFESSION PRAYER

(based on Romans 10:10; James 5:16; I John 1:7-9, 3:8)

"Lord Jesus, I believe that You are the Son of God. You are the Messiah, come in the flesh to destroy the works of the devil. You died on the cross for my sins and rose again the third day from the dead. I now confess all my sins and repent. I receive your forgiveness and ask you to cleanse me from all sin. Thank You for redeeming me, cleansing me, justifying me, and sanctifying me in Your blood."

FORGIVENESS PRAYER

(based on Matthew 6:14-15; Leviticus 19:18)

"Lord, I have a confession to make. I have not loved, but have resented certain people and have unforgiveness in my heart. I call upon You, Lord, to help me forgive them. I do now forgive (name them). I also forgive and accept myself in the name of Jesus Christ."

PRIDE PRAYER

(based on Proverbs 11:2, 16:18, 26:12; 1 Timothy 3:6)

"Father, I come to You in the name of the Lord Jesus Christ. I know pride is an abomination to You. I renounce anything that would cause me to have pride in my heart in dealing with other people. I renounce these and turn away from them. I humble myself before You and come to You as a little child."

Study Proverbs 6:16-19 and remember that fasting is a means by which a person humbles himself before the Lord.

GENERATIONAL BONDAGE PRAYER

(based on Exodus 20:4-6, 34:7; Numbers 14:18)

"In the name of the Lord Jesus Christ, I now renounce, break, and loose myself from all bondages or bonds of physical or mental illness upon me, my family or family line as the result of parents or any other ancestors. I thank You, Lord, for setting me free."

Notes.

John G. Lake. *The Collected Works Of John G.*

David O. Oyedepo (1995). *The Blood Triumph.* Dominion Publishing House, Nigeria.

Johannes, Battle In The Sea.

Prayer Journal Spring 14_V7.indd 20 12/4/15 2:40 PM

Quin Sherrer And Ruthanne Garlock (2010) *The Spiritual Warrior's Prayer Guide: Find Your Breakthrough In Any Situation,* Regal Books: USA.

DR H. Clifton Black. *Deliverance And Demonic Oppression: Whatever You Bind On Earth Will Be Bound On Earth.*

Don't miss out!

Visit the website below and you can sign up to receive emails whenever Johannes Tefo publishes a new book. There's no charge and no obligation.

https://books2read.com/r/B-A-UEZX-YKHBD

BOOKS2READ

Connecting independent readers to independent writers.

Did you love *Freedom: Deliverance Of Souls From Captivity*? Then you should read *Battle In The Sea: How To Tackle Spiritual Warfare And Win The Battle*[1] by Johannes Tefo!

[2]

This is a must-have book about how to tackle spiritual warfare and win in the name of the LORD. Through this profound book, you will come out armed with strategic prayers to silence the powers that have been harassing' and messing with your life. The marine kingdom is one of the deadliest kingdoms of Satan, located under the sea. This book came through a revelation. As someone who has been the victim of evil, as we all are, the LORD has been gracious to me, teaching my hands how to wage the right warfare against

---

1. https://books2read.com/u/49aE5X

2. https://books2read.com/u/49aE5X

the enemy. Through years of experience and the work of the Holy Spirit, this is the book to amplify your inner man and strengthen you in times like this. Believers have to take territory, win souls, and deliver captives, this is a must-have book filled with wisdom and knowledge for your spiritual deliverance.

Also by Johannes Tefo

Family spiritual Warfare Books

Generational Curses And Spiritual Warfare: Spiritual Strategies & Principles Of Victory Against Evil Strongholds

Youth's Guide To Spiritual Warfare

A Women's Guide To Spiritual Warfare

Standalone

Deliver Your Soul From Evil

Overcoming Spirit Of Stagnation

The 24: Prophetic Word For This Season 2024 And Beyond

Michael For Warfare

Territorial Spirits: Overcome Evil Strongholds in Your Life And Take Over Your Community With Strategic Warfare And Winning Prayers

Prayers Against Suicide Spirit

Spiritual Warfare When Enough is Enough

Identity In Christ

Prayers Against Satanic Networks

The Workplace You Need: Spiritual Warfare Prayers That Silence Evil Powers At Your Workplace.

Deliverance From Mind Control: Be Free And Delivered From Every Marine Demons Of Mind Control

Times Getting Hard: Scriptures Of Comfort For Hard Days

Battle In The Sea: How To Tackle Spiritual Warfare And Win The Battle

Freedom: Deliverance Of Souls From Captivity

About the Author

Before he started writing Christian books, Johannes got a graduate degree in Film and Television from university of Johannesburg. After that, just to shake things up, he went to equip himself with religious studies, particularly Christianity, just to have knack about the world beyond the curtains of time. And how this body of Christ has transformed millions of people around the world, not neglecting how sadly the movement has been persecuted from time to time. He now writes full time.